Being Adopted

Amy Wilkerson, LCSW

Fulton Books, Inc.
Meadville, PA

Published by Fulton Books 2021

ISBN 978-1-63710-972-4 (paperback)
ISBN 978-1-63860-088-6 (hardcover)
ISBN 978-1-63710-973-1 (digital)

Printed in the United States of America

To my birth mother, Angela, and my adoptive parents Mary, Mel, and Cindy. Thank you for each showing me how to live in your own powerful and beautiful ways.

For my children, Talia, Aiden, and Amaya. Thank you for being my greatest teachers and brightest lights.

For my husband, Matthew. Thank you for showing me what unconditional means and for being my biggest champion.

Being adopted means you no longer live with your biological parents and have joined another family through a legal process.

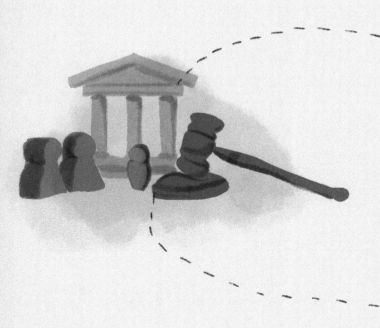

Lots of kids all around the world are adopted just like you.

Some adoptees never knew their biological families.

Other adoptees lived with their biological families before meeting their adoptive families.

Some adopted kids share a race and ethnicity with their adoptive families.

Others have a different race or ethnicity than their adoptive families. They are known as transracial adoptees.

Some adoptive parents are married.

Some are single.

Some adoptees have two daddies.

Some adoptees have two mommies.

Some adoptees know a lot about their stories and why they were adopted.

Others do not have any details at all.

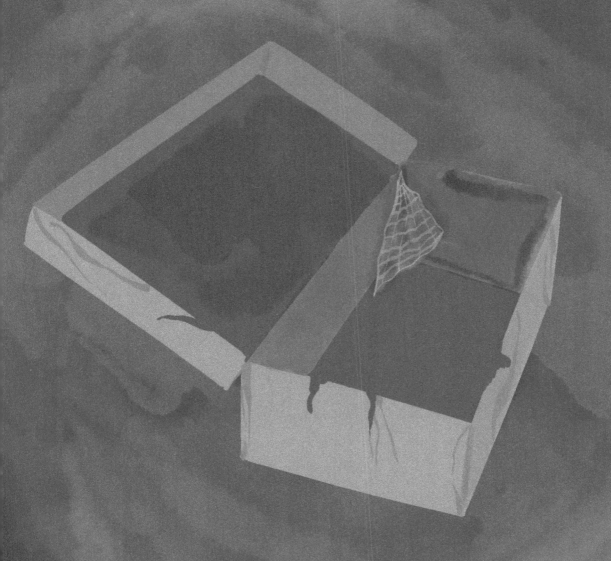

Some adopted kids live in the city.

Some live in the country.

No matter where you live, no matter who you live with...

Adoption can bring a mixture of thoughts and feelings.

16

It is normal to feel sad about not being able to live with your biological family. It is normal to feel sad about living with your adoptive family.

It is normal to feel happy you are no longer living with your biological family. It is normal to feel happy you are living with your adoptive family.

Being adopted means you have lost many things.

LAST SUMMER

Being adopted means you have gained many things.

On some days you may want to talk a lot about your adoption and on other days you may not. Both are normal.

Where are you from?

Do you know who your **REAL** parents are?

Do you want to find your **REAL** family?

You should never have to answer questions or be forced to talk about your adoption if you are not comfortable. These are your stories, and you get to share them when and how you want.

One day, you may want to find your biological family.

Search

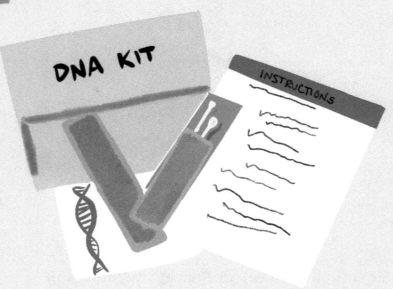

DNA KIT

INSTRUCTIONS

This may or may not be possible.

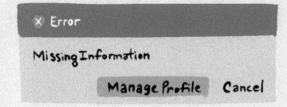

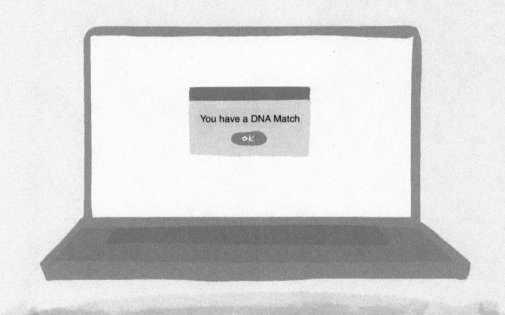

Whether your biological family is or is not in your life, they created you.
What parts of you do you think come from them?

You are a beautiful blend of your biological family, adoptive family, and the unique and special force that is YOU!

Being adopted means you have already lived through so much.

Being adopted means you are strong, resilient, and capable of great things, even on the days when you do not feel like it.

How you feel about your adoption will grow and change over time just like your body grows and changes.

INSERT AN
IMAGE OF
YOU!

7 inches

5 inches

Being adopted is a part of your story. You matter. No matter how you came into this world, no matter how you joined your family, You ARE MEANT TO BE.

Caregiver Guide

Creating a family through the process of adoption is an emotional and meaningful journey. Raising adopted children means parents and caregivers must be prepared and equipped with the knowledge, resources, and compassion to best support the evolving adoptee identity. Too often, the absence of pre-adoption education or lack of emphasis on post-adoption resources leaves the complexities and traumas adoptees carry with them unexplored or minimized. Without the proper tools to process, it can be harder for adoptees to manage positive identity formation. To create emotionally productive and healing spaces, we must acknowledge love is not always enough when raising adopted children. How we talk to children about their adoption and adoption, in general, can have profound and long-lasting effects on how adoptees process and conceptualize their purpose, self-worth, and self-esteem. I have created this guide as a tool for caregivers when diving into adoption-related conversations.

For *all* adoptees, their attachment has been disrupted, and a trauma has occurred. The extent and impact of the trauma should *always* be defined by the adoptee's perception of their own loss and it can be ever-evolving. As a parent or caregiver, you can help your adoptee navigate their emotions by creating a nonjudgmental, nonbiased, open, and loving environment. Being an adoptive parent or caregiver is being a trauma-informed parent or caregiver. Often in my work as a social worker or in clinical practice, many adoptive parents express hesitation and insecurity when it comes to discussing their child's adoption with their adoptee. However, the natural desire to protect and shelter children from pain often overshadows opportunities to grow meaningful attachment and practice resiliency. The absence of validation can isolate an adoptee and ultimately jeopardize the ability and need to feel secure and safe in their adoption journey. I do not want those moments to go unseized for any adoptive parent or caregiver. I want to help cultivate and encourage moments to grow and heal together in your home.

My goal from the beginning was to create a book any adoptee could pick up and see themselves within the pages. The universal truths of grief, loss, and trauma resonate in all adoption narratives no matter specific details. Whether your adoptee verbalizes their questions or feelings surrounding their adoption, I would caution against making any assumptions that it is not on their mind. Being adopted can be a very isolating and complex experience and if parents and caregivers are not intentional about creating and holding spaces for adoptees to freely process and express themselves, adoptees will often create their own conclusions about their place and worth in the world.

If you are a caregiver reading this book with your adoptee, note the following:

- *Listen.* Listening is one of the most validating tools parents and caregivers can utilize in supporting adoptees. Giving adoptees the space to process their thoughts and feelings without interruption or questioning gives the adoptee the chance to learn how to express themselves freely without censorship or pressure. Listening without thinking of a response is also impactful as it allows you to focus on the content of what your adoptee is saying without needing to fix or pivot the conversation.
- *Validate.* Like anything else, thoughts and feelings can change on a single topic over a lifetime. It is okay to ask the adoptee how they feel as they turn the pages of this book, but there should be no pressure for them to answer or provide an answer. Whether your adoptee offers their thoughts and feelings or not, acknowledge how brave, hard, confusing, and/or overwhelming, it can be to engage in these conversations.
- *Honor.* Acknowledging a conversation is one thing, but to honor the conversation takes your validation a step further. Letting an adoptee know their feelings are normal helps adopted children feel seen and heard. Using affirming statements such as "That would be hard for me" or "I might

struggle if _____" helps the adoptee also know there is worth in their feelings, and they are not the only one who may be feeling a particular way.

- *Answer questions with honesty,* It is okay if you do not have an answer to a question your adoptee may ask. Always lead adoption conversations with honesty. Creating a scenario that seems less painful only will create more confusion and pain for your adoptee in the long run. Statements such as "Your birth parents loved you so much they wanted you to have a better life" do not heal lived experiences or make emotions easier to hold. There are numerous reasons why children are placed for adoption. Now more than ever, we need to be cautious and mindful that our statements do not promote classism, racism, or other systems of oppression that imply the group your child comes from is incapable of raising or caring for their children. It is imperative as an adoptive parent you continue to seek ongoing education and constantly challenge your own thoughts, feelings, and perceptions on these topics.

- *Do not take your adoptee's feelings personal,* It can be hard to acknowledge, but there is a piece of your adopted child's story that does not include you as the parent or caregiver. They have biological ties to another family that is rooted in its own culture and history. In the same way parents can love more than one child, children are capable of loving more than one set of parents. Loving, missing, or craving connection with biological family is not always a reflection on adoptive familial support or love but rather a natural and normal physiological process adoptees work through over the lifespan.

- *Process your emotions away from your adoptee,* Always be mindful of how your adoptee is processing their adoption and your own patterns. If you are feeling the need or want to fix, change, or sugarcoat your adoptee's feelings, be sure to process these prompts away from your adoptee in a safe and loving place. Just like adoption is a complex journey for your adoptee, adoption is a complex journey for adoptive parents and caregivers as well.

As your adoptee grows and changes, so will you. Whether it's topics of race, biological family, deserving versus undeserving, family preservation, religion, culture, reunion, or policies and politics, several events can influence how you view your child's adoption. Keeping your own bias in check is one of the best gifts you can give your adoptee. Helping them see their birth family and culture in a positive light helps them see the same worth in themselves. When parents or caregivers have not processed their own triggers or patterns, the pressure and burden often gets placed on the adopted child.

As you continue to navigate the adoption experience, may you always continue to seek education, support, and remember you are not alone. Thank you for using this book as a tool and guide for your adoptee. It is an honor to be part of your family's journey.

Best wishes always in body, mind, and spirit.

Amy Wilkerson, LCSW
@growhealblossom
www.growhealblossom.com

Book Reviews

Factual and clear, this book provides clear support and acceptance for a wide range of situations and families. No child will be left out of this narrative; Amy includes them all! Your adopted child will close this book feeling seen, heard, and worthy.

—Brittany S., adoptive mother

While all families can connect with something in this book, it should be on *every* adoptive family's bookshelf. I know it is intended to be a children's book, but the "you matter" message connects with me as an adult adoptee! I actually wish I'd had this book as a small child when I was trying to process big feelings about being adopted.

—Angela O., transracial Colombian adoptee

This book provides a great opportunity for adoptive parents to begin an important and, often, lifelong internal dialogue within an adoptee about what it means to be adopted. As an adoptee, I wish this book had been around when I was young enough to have my parents read this to me! Its messages are easy for young minds to grasp, despite discussing such a serious topic. Throughout this book, adoptees are taught that they are part of a larger community—a community that includes adoptees and families from all walks of life; and that all of this is normal. It encourages self-exploration of both who the adoptee is personally and the emotions that come with being adopted. A must-have for adoptive parents of young children!

—Jim M., transracial and international adoptee

This book normalizes so many emotions for children and families who are navigating the journey of adoption. It brought tears to my eyes to read the simple, yet profound truths captured so beautifully. Even now, as an adult adoptee who has spent years digging down deep and doing the hard work of owning and understanding her story, I feel comfort, strength, and a *knowing* as I read this book. I wish I had a tool like this as a child and am excited to share it with my own children one day.

—Heidi, adoptee and LPC

Amy really captured the mixed feelings adoptees feel when thinking about their identity and their story. I wish my parents had access to a book like this while I was growing up. This book is an incredible resource for adoptive families and children; it will help assist conversations and reflections needed for healthy adoptive family development.

—Maria T., LMHC, LPC Therapist and
a Transracial and International Adoptee

About the Illustrators

Caleb Yee (전영호)

A Korean-American adoptee located in Southern California, for the last five years, Caleb has been creating artwork that personifies the adoptee's voice through a variety of colors, symbolism, and cultural influences related to the adoptee experience. His artwork vision is to invite his audience into space where they can insert themselves into the artist's experience and feel validated or perhaps even challenged. It is the thought process, use of vivid imagination, and personal story that continue to propel and inspire the artist's journey. Caleb has participated in numerous art exhibitions in Los Angeles, California, and has made many art-related contributions to adoption-related organizations domestically and internationally. Currently, his aspirations include pursuing a career in art therapy as well as providing his community with space where they can express themselves and their stories through creative means.

Website: www.calebyeeartwork.com
Instagram: www.instagram.com/calebyeeartwork

Erin Kim

Erin Kim is an illustrator who loves her work as it evolves with each new personal and professional project. She specializes in digital illustration from portraits to sneakers to Korean food. Her work has been published in *Edible Memphis* and for numerous issues of *Barista Magazine*. Erin is also a Korean adoptee who has written about her experience at *INHERITANCE Magazine* and spoken on numerous panels regarding the transracial international adoptee narrative. She hopes to continue creating work that is relevant to adoptees as the marginalized conversation becomes more universally sought after.

When she's not drawing, Erin is spending time with her partner, James, and malamute pup, Yuna. They hope to travel more in the future and eat all the yummy foods.

Personal: @oneofakim7
Illustrator: @inkandkimchi_

CPSIA information can be obtained
at www.ICGtesting.com
Printed in the USA
LVHW070920300122
709772LV00007B/155